THE PEARLS OF LIFE

UNIVERSAL SONNETS

KONDA MURALI

Copyright © Konda Murali
All Rights Reserved.

This book has been self-published with all reasonable efforts taken to make the material error-free by the author. No part of this book shall be used, reproduced in any manner whatsoever without written permission from the author, except in the case of brief quotations embodied in critical articles and reviews.

The Author of this book is solely responsible and liable for its content including but not limited to the views, representations, descriptions, statements, information, opinions and references ["Content"]. The Content of this book shall not constitute or be construed or deemed to reflect the opinion or expression of the Publisher or Editor. Neither the Publisher nor Editor endorse or approve the Content of this book or guarantee the reliability, accuracy or completeness of the Content published herein and do not make any representations or warranties of any kind, express or implied, including but not limited to the implied warranties of merchantability, fitness for a particular purpose. The Publisher and Editor shall not be liable whatsoever for any errors, omissions, whether such errors or omissions result from negligence, accident, or any other cause or claims for loss or damages of any kind, including without limitation, indirect or consequential loss or damage arising out of use, inability to use, or about the reliability, accuracy or sufficiency of the information contained in this book.

Made with ♥ on the Notion Press Platform
www.notionpress.com

To all my well-wishers,

This work is dedicated to you, the guiding lights in my life who have stood by me through every twist and turn, from the serene beauty of nature to the peculiar challenges of new beginnings. Your unwavering support and belief in my dreams have been the pillars that held me strong, especially during those times when I found myself in unfamiliar territories, be it the edge of a dangerous barrage or the chaos of city life.

To those who understood my silent tears and the deep emotions I poured into my writings, your empathy has been my refuge. To those who encouraged my passion for literature, my heartfelt gratitude for allowing me to explore and express my soul through words.

Thank you for being my constant companions in this journey, for believing in my vision, and for inspiring me to persevere. This book is as much yours as it is mine.

With deepest appreciation,
Konda Murali Author & Poet

9441431090

Contents

Acknowledgements ix

Prologue xi

1. The Weight Of Absence 1
2. The Gift Of Friendship 2
3. The Confession 3
4. The Nature Of True Love 4
5. The Strength Of Women 6
6. Fortune In Love 7
7. Ode To Mother 8
8. The Measure Of Fatherhood 9
9. The Essence Of Life 11
10. The Tools Of Triumph 12
11. The Path Through Challenges 13
12. The Art Of Apology 14
13. The Art Of Prioritizing 15
14. The Path To Growth 16
15. The Pursuit Of Peace 17
16. The Nature Of Solitude 18
17. The Power Of Repentance 19
18. The Value Of Time 20
19. The True Essence Of Family 21
20. The Roots Of Ego 22
21. The Impermanence Of Life 23
22. The Power Of Reading 25

Contents

23. The Melody Of Music	26
24. A Discourse Of Broken Promises	27
25. The Nature Of Love	28
26. The Solace In Absence	30
27. The Shifting Heart	31
28. The Strain Of Unkindness	32
29. A Birthday's Blissful Glow	33
30. The Depths Of Unspoken Love	34
31. The Chains Of Existence	35
32. The Inner Warrior	36
33. The Lessons Of Tears	37
34. The True Nature Of Love	38
35. Transformation Through Love	39
36. The Agony Of Unfulfilled Love	41
37. The Eternal Bond Of Two Souls	43
38. The True Essence Of Love	44
39. The Agony Of Waiting	45
40. The Soul's Enduring Pain	46
41. A Souvenir Of Life's Transformation	47
42. The Rarest Eyes	48
43. The Wounds Of A Broken Heart	49
44. The Test Of Time And Love	50
45. The Trial Of The Heart	52
46. The Rose Of Love	53

Contents

47. The Call For Change — 54
48. The Weight Of Unyielding Pain — 55
49. The Melancholy Of Unmet Affection — 56
50. When Fantasy Becomes Reality — 57

Acknowledgements

To all my well-wishers,

This work is dedicated to you—the guiding lights in my life who have stood by me through every twist and turn, from the serene beauty of nature to the peculiar challenges of new beginnings. Your unwavering support and belief in my dreams have been the pillars that held me strong, especially during those times when I found myself in unfamiliar territories, be it the edge of a dangerous barrage or the chaos of city life.

I would like to express my sincere gratitude to my dear friends and family members. Your encouragement and support have been invaluable in helping me complete this book. Additionally, my heartfelt thanks go out to my students and colleagues, whose promise and encouragement have been a constant source of inspiration.

To those who understood my silent tears and the deep emotions I poured into my writings, your empathy has been my refuge. To those who encouraged my passion for literature, my deepest appreciation for allowing me to explore and express my soul through words.

Thank you for being my constant companions in this journey, for believing in my vision, and for inspiring me to persevere. This book is as much yours as it is mine.

Konda Murali

Prologue

The Pearls of Life

    I am Konda Murali, teacher and scribe,
With five books penned, my passion brought to light,
The fifth, "The Pearls of Life," where customs thrive,
In sonnets formed with wisdom's guiding might.

    A dream I held, to craft in verse a tome,
Where Indian culture's depth and grace unfold,
One hundred sonnets from the heart and home,
In varied styles, the ancient tales retold.

    In Shakespeare's pattern, fifty pearls align,
With twenty-five in Spenser's structured rhyme,
The rest, Petrarchan, timeless, they define
A culture rich, enduring through all time.

    From life's experience, this book took shape,
A tribute to the wisdom I now drape.

1. The Weight of Absence

Your absence fills my heart with silent pain,
I count the days until you're here once more,
Each day a century, a time so plain,
I watch the clock, my eyes forever sore.

I listen to the songs you softly sung,
To soothe the ache that lingers in my chest,
I recollect the days when love was young,
And whisper of the joys that we possessed.

I dream of all the talks we used to share,
Elated by sweet thoughts of what we knew,
Remembering the crush, beyond compare,
Yet deep within, I mourn the sad adieu.

These memories, though cherished, are not real,
I sigh and wake, returning to the real.

2. The Gift of Friendship

Friendship lifts the weight of stress we bear,
It brightens life and fills our days with light,
A friend's kind care and love are always there,
Their presence makes our world feel safe and right.

A friend will stand beside us through the strife,
With unconditional support so true,
They guard our secrets, lift us in our life,
And guide us when the shadows cloud our view.

A friend won't leave us lost in times of woe,
Their loyalty is steadfast, pure, and clear,
In every deed, they let their kindness show,
And with their praise, they banish every fear.

Though miles apart, a friend will always stay,
Their heart remains with us, no time or space can sway.

3. The Confession

I wrote my love in words, a pure confession,
Admiring her, her beauty, thoughts, and grace,
With joy, I drove to give my true expression,
She took it shyly, blush upon her face.

No hard copy, so a picture I kept,
A secret file within my phone concealed,
Her praise soon had me soaring, joy adept,
The thrill of love and passion was revealed.

But soon the truth emerged, her mother read,
And fear took hold, the tale was quickly spread,
Her father warned, my heart was filled with dread,
I faced the storm that reckless love had bred.

From this, I learned a lesson harsh and true,
Impulses unchecked bring grief to you.

4. The Nature of True Love

In reel life, love appears with just a glance,
A fleeting moment, beauty's quick allure,
But real love grows through time and shared expanse,
Through conversations deep, sincere, and pure.

True love is more than passion's fleeting flame,
It's showing care that never fades away,
Unconditional and free of blame,
Respect and trust are what it will convey.

Love isn't gazing into eyes alone,
It's seeing life with one united view,
Lust seeks the form, but love is deeply grown,
It craves the joy that makes two hearts renew.

At last, true love commits with steadfast will,
With values shared, together standing still.

5. The Strength of Women

Women are caretakers and contributors,
They lead in fields, in factories, and more,
As professionals, athletes, and laborers,
In every role, they thrive and help restore.

They plan the meals that nourish every home,
And guide the economy with wisdom's hand,
As better halves, they shape the earth they roam,
Long-term developers of this proud land.

Creators of new life, they stand with grace,
Supporting change, they drive the world ahead,
We must respect their strength in every space,
And build them up, not let their spirits shed.

Though challenges arise, they won't give way,
They turn the trials to growth and light the day.

6. Fortune in Love

Finding and meeting you, my fortune's grace,
The days we share are memories so sweet,
My soul takes flight each time I see your face,
And in that thrill, my heart and spirit meet.

Each day with you is filled with endless thrill,
Fantasies within me take to flight,
Even when we argue, joy fills me still,
For in your soul, I find my pure delight.

May blessings come to you from heavens high,
With leisure, strength in virtue, wisdom's might,
With patience through all trials life may try,
And courage strong to face each daunting fight.

What joy it is to love, my heart does sing,
For in your love, I find my everything.

7. Ode to Mother

By hearing "mother," feelings overflow,
A surge of deep emotions, pure and true,
She plays a role that all our lives do know,
Forgiving, gentle, always seeing through.

A mother is the symbol of pure love,
She gives her joy for others' needs above,
With pride and honor, she will always serve,
Her care a gift, a blessing from above.

God, not everywhere, created her,
A being so divine, so kind, so near,
A counselor, a friend who can confer,
And sense the worries that we hold so dear.

My mother is my guide, my shining light,
Blessed am I, with her love, pure and bright.

8. The Measure of Fatherhood

Becoming a father is an easy claim,
Yet proving it requires a lifetime's test,
What fatherhood truly means, you come to name,
Through trials faced, your strength and love expressed.

A father's struggle is often unseen,
His worries and his hurdles, masked from view,
He may not inspire in the ways we've dreamed,
Yet through his life, his lessons will come through.

He won't dictate how you should lead your way,
Instead, he lives and shows you how to strive,
In midlife's reflection, you'll come to say,
His life's example helped you to survive.

THE PEARLS OF LIFE

I am so blessed to be a son so true,
To my fantastic father, guiding through.

9. The Essence of Life

Our birth is fleeting as a single beat,
And death, a whisper in that same short span,
Between these moments, life's trials and feats,
A heaven's paradox, where beauty can.

Alone we come, and alone we depart,
Craving fleeting things that life can bring,
We live with haste, our purpose left apart,
Creating chaos with each yearning fling.

Life's like an ice cream, savor it with zest,
Before it melts away with fleeting grace,
We think death's distant, so we live unblessed,
Acting without thought, in the time we chase.

Life's a gift from God, so cherish every day,
Live fully, with purpose, in every way.

10. The Tools of Triumph

To play until you're spent—that's just a game,
To fight till victory is yours—combat's claim,
In life's grand scheme, existence takes its frame,
Reside until you fade, yet still proclaim.

A sword may help you vanquish foes with might,
A brood may earn the sympathy of hearts,
But if a book becomes your guiding light,
It wins the world and all its varied parts.

If happiness once known seems now afar,
And past days shine more brightly than today,
Perhaps past trials cast a stronger scar,
Though it seemed the best in every way.

Embrace the present, for it's not a flaw,
In this sonnet, find the truth of all.

11. The Path Through Challenges

Where there is love, there comes a trial's test,
And with that trial, pain may surely rise,
Yet through the hardship and the aching quest,
A heart with fervent will will find its prize.

Life's problems come to each, it's truth we face,
Respecting these, we navigate with care,
We tread with caution, seeking success's grace,
And strive with keen resolve, our dreams laid bare.

Direct your mind to focus on the bright,
On positives that help the soul to grow,
Rather than dwell on shadows of the night,
Find strength in hope, let only good things show.

Great souls don't falter in the face of strife,
They rise and grow, so keep on through the life.

12. The Art of Apology

To say "sorry" doesn't mean you're at fault,
But shows you value those you wish to aid,
It's offering respect, not a default,
A way to mend the bonds that may have swayed.

Let not your words cause wounds upon the soul,
For tender spirits break with harsh, cruel speech,
Preserve the freedom in each heartfelt role,
And mend the fractured feelings you might breach.

Had I not erred, my place might be more high,
Yet in my striving, I've sought the best I can,
To improve, I learn from each mistake's cry,
And aim for greatness, guided by this plan.

Patience tames the fury, goodness soothes the tear,
In mastering these, the heart finds paths more clear.

13. The Art of Prioritizing

Some choices made in life may come undone,
Instead of dwelling on what's past, be wise,
Embrace the present with optimism,
And focus on what truly helps you rise.

Prioritizing is the key to thrive,
Without it, success remains afar,
When objects not essential take your time,
The crucial things may not be seen or star.

If education holds the greatest worth,
Then place it high above all else and more,
Neglecting it for triviality's mirth,
Means losing out on what you can't restore.

So discern what matters most to you,
And place aside what's less significant too.

14. The Path to Growth

At first, we work for mere survival's sake,
And as we progress, we seek to rise above,
Striving for better, our own path to make,
Enhancing ourselves with a free spirit's love.

Avoid the comfort zone where ease resides,
For staying still won't lead to evolution,
In familiarity, strength often hides,
Unseen, as we miss the growth's true solution.

Strength emerges when we face life's trials,
Embrace each day as a challenge to meet,
In the struggle, reality unveils,
And change appears where we dare to compete.

Life offers many paths beyond the safe,
Embrace the risks to find the growth you crave.

15. The Pursuit of Peace

Even with goals achieved, peace eludes me still,
And hope persists that it will never fade,
Though I may rise, no crown my efforts fill,
I choose to work with perseverance laid.

I've shed many tears, a torrent of despair,
No one to comfort through my deepest plight,
In my sorrows, few have shown they care,
Yet through the pain, I strive to see the light.

Life's course is beyond our grasp, it's true,
Birth and death are not ours to command,
The choice we have is how we live our view,
To make our days as grand as we had planned.

Mistakes are part of ardent human strive,
In life's great scheme, it's common to revive.

16. The Nature of Solitude

We seek out friends to chase away our pain,
Yet loneliness is deep within the soul,
It's not just being alone in the domain,
But feeling low, with confidence not whole.

If strength is found within, though one is lone,
It's called self-confidence, not solitude,
Some dwell among the crowd yet feel unknown,
Their attitude low, their mood subdued.

Some thrive in solitude, with self-belief,
Their confidence high, though they are single,
While others, in the crowd, seek no relief,
Their inner state remains a quiet tingle.

At times, to be alone can bring one peace,
And at times, the world's company can cease.

17. The Power of Repentance

To feel regret for past missteps is sweet relief,
It heals the heart and soothes the soul's deep pain,
Without such feelings, one may bring more grief,
Continuing to hurt, causing others' strain.

It's wise to engage in life's games with grace,
Yet never play with hearts, for charm's deceit,
For games with people often leave a trace,
Of sadness lingering where joy should meet.

If betrayal strikes, it's best to step away,
Such distance serves as justice, firm and true,
For misunderstanding is not worth the fray,
Appreciation is due, in all we do.

Repentance is not sorrow, but a start,
To halt lamenting and to change the heart.

18. The Value of Time

Some lead their lives with careless, distant eyes,
Believing there's naught to be done or sought,
When questioned, they respond with somber sighs,
As if demise is where their fate is caught.

Time, the essence of our fleeting span,
Is life itself, a truth we must embrace,
No one can know what lies beyond this plan,
So strive to make each moment hold its place.

Procrastination breeds a life of woe,
It sparks anxiety and stress so dire,
Goals slip away, and health begins to show,
Destruction follows when we don't aspire.

So cast aside the complaints and the delay,
Be kind, keep learning, and seize each day.

19. The True Essence of Family

Family is not a mere collection of kin,
But a cluster of emotions deeply shared,
Defined not by blood but by love within,
A bond of mutual care, always prepared.

In family, we voice our deepest woes,
Their hearts are open, guiding us with hope,
They steer us toward a brighter path that shows,
And help us in our lives to better cope.

This love is vital for our well-being's grace,
It molds our hearts and shapes our inner core,
In tender care, each member finds their place,
And kindness blooms where affection is sure.

As the old saying wisdom does impart,
"A child is the father of the man" at heart.

20. The Roots of Ego

Insecurity breeds ego's silent reign,
It drains our will, distorts our view of truth,
Creating myths where real thoughts are in vain,
And leads us to conjectures, far from proof.

Ego's grip has many harsh effects,
It severs bonds with those of worthy grace,
Desire to conquer and collect deflects,
And feedback's voice is lost, misplaced, erased.

To tame this ego, learn to praise the best,
Seek help when needed, and embrace critique,
Celebrate others' wins, let modesty attest,
To openness and honesty, be meek.

Manage emotions with understanding clear,
In truth and humility, we find our steer.

21. The Impermanence of Life

O man, O man, one day you must depart,
From Earth's embrace, you'll leave your mortal place,
Why not cherish each moment, play your part?
Live contentedly till death's quiet grace.

Life's span is fleeting, yet it holds such worth,
Your birth was unique, a chance so rare,
Don't squander this precious gift upon the earth,
For it is not eternal, but transient air.

Leave a mark upon this world with deeds so grand,
Make your name resonate through time and fame,
Understand the virtue in creation's hand,
Death is certain, and that's life's solemn claim.

Invented wonders in this vast expanse,
Yet forgotten how to live, to truly dance.

22. The Power of Reading

Reading shapes us into better forms,
It molds our minds with values rich and deep,
With broad perspectives, in its pages warms,
A book reveals the truths that wisdom keeps.

Through stories, we embark on journeys vast,
With characters whose lives we come to know,
Their trials and triumphs shape our hearts at last,
And through their paths, our inner strength does grow.

The benefits are many, it's quite clear,
It sharpens minds, enhances empathy,
Reduces stress and helps us sleep more near,
With vocabulary growing endlessly.

Though wealth may elude, let reading be your guide,
It's a treasure found within, your heart's own pride.

23. The Melody of Music

Music is the soul's true, nourishing food,
Reflecting moods and elevating hearts,
A music teacher shapes the soothing tune,
Crafting melodies as life's finest arts.

Musicians bless us with their heartfelt strains,
Their notes weave harmony, rhythm, and grace,
Creating joy, where melody remains,
A raga's theme in every heartfelt phrase.

Music reigns supreme, invoking deep emotion,
With moods it molds, a symphony of feeling,
Though unplanned, its notation finds devotion,
In teaching tunes, its purest art revealing.

Music speaks in ways profound and grand,
Enjoy its gifts, and health will take a stand.

24. A Discourse of Broken Promises

How shall I compare you, my dear soul,
When this is not the way to treat a heart?
Do you not grasp the depth of my own role?
Do you only think of your own part?

Have you forgotten our vows, once so true?
When you pledged our union would last for all,
Where is that promise, that bond we knew?
Now every day, disputes make our hearts fall.

I've borne with patience, silence my refrain,
Yet you present choices that drive me mad.
I, too, am human, prone to anger's strain,
Why do you ignore me, make me feel so sad?

For your whims, you seek, while I face the test,
Where is our pact? The love we once possessed?

25. The Nature of Love

Love's essence may elude the eyes of those
We cherish most, our feelings masked and veiled,
What's shown may not be genuine, who knows?
And what's concealed, yet not by charlatan hailed.

Love is the same for rich and humble hearts,
Like fire, wind, sky, water, earth's embrace,
A layman's love may not be wealth's fine art,
A rich man's may flaunt its material grace.

To watchers, beauty's surface can suffice,
Aesthetic hearts admire the craft and skill,
Yet true affection's depth is not so nice,
It's shunned, while adoration is fulfilled.

In love's pure form, the heart remains sincere,
Beyond the guise, true love's intent is clear.

KONDA MURALI

26. The Solace in Absence

Missing a close heart brings its own shame,
Yet sleep soothes the suffering and the ache,
In dreams, that heart appears, a gentle flame,
Rest becomes the balm for the absence we take.

From afar, all seems lovely, free from flaw,
The view is splendid when we climb up high,
Fire's warmth, from distance, is without awe,
But up close, it burns, and makes us shy.

So longing for someone may be a grace,
When pain strikes, seek solace in other ways,
Sleep and dreams offer a cherished embrace,
Where absent hearts appear in soft arrays.

In distance, we find comfort's gentle art,
In dreams, we meet the closeness of the heart.

27. The Shifting Heart

A lovely lady had a learned love,
Everything thrived until the lockdown's grip,
Her fondness for him fell like winter's shove,
Gradually, her heart began to slip.

To her, he was once friend and all in one,
Now he stands as enemy, rival cold,
The silence grew where once the warmth had spun,
Though he remains blank, his intentions bold.

The sudden shift brought him deep concern,
While she, in her new light, lives carefree,
His worry turned to quiet acceptance,
He chose to let her live, set her free.

For love's true nature is to give and go,
Even when it leads to sorrow's woe.

28. The Strain of Unkindness

Why don't you show kindness? This isn't a bond,
Why this torment? Don't you seek to mature?
Why target me with words so far beyond,
What do you want? Your bluntness is obscure.

Why do you persist in questioning me?
I sense your queries like a piercing pain,
Do you only think of your own plea,
While I feel you neither care nor sustain?

How long will this discord continue to flare?
I see you now as nothing but a foe,
Your behavior feels like a harsh snare,
I warn you now to not appear and show.

For kindness lost can sever ties so deep,
And in its wake, only discord will we reap.

29. A Birthday's Blissful Glow

Birthdays shine with beauty and delight,
When soulmates craft surprises, tender and true,
The day's bright hours are never in blight,
Unlike summer's peak where warmth bids adieu.

The kisses spark with joy, a kingfisher's flight,
Conversations drift like chariots in grand,
Eateries brim with cheer on this night,
While drinks toast the love that forever stands.

The party soothes and comforts the dear one,
Gifts bring grace, and gratitude's embrace,
Sweetheart's warmth, with hospitality spun,
Ensures the pleasure of this cherished place.

Thus, the party preserves joy's endless sheen,
In memories made, where love is evergreen.

30. The Depths of Unspoken Love

Feel the feelings that within you lie,
Not just the person you keep in mind,
You may not grasp what makes her soul sigh,
Yet her essence is what you'll come to find.

You may see her faults where none exist,
Even when her heart is pure and true,
Yet love's depth is not always dismissed,
For adoring her madly is what you do.

Though consequences may arise from this,
And harsh words may be spoken in strife,
Your honesty is known in the abyss,
And she may understand, post the turmoil of life.

For deep love's truths often come to light
When damage is done, and wrongs are made right.

31. The Chains of Existence

The memories linger, refuse to fade,
Duties weigh heavily, deny release,
Rights bind our tongues, leave no words unsaid,
Morals restrain our steps, seeking peace.

Ethics curtail our labor's might,
Values disallow violence to reign,
Preaches silence our soothing respite,
While conflicts prevent us from easing pain.

Songs fail to stir a deepened sense,
Books promise growth yet leave us incomplete,
Movies shape us, yet still, we're not immense,
In the quest for joy, all seems obsolete.

For nothing seems to grant true cheer,
Bound by life's chains, happiness remains unclear.

32. The Inner Warrior

In this vast world, each soul a warrior stands,
Unseen battles rage within the heart's core,
No victory banners, no external bands,
Yet the fiercest fight lies at the spirit's door.

The clash is silent, where no voices ring,
A fight with shadows deep in the mind's keep,
Where sabotage lurks, a most perilous thing,
The war within, where restless souls do weep.

It steals our peace, ignites a ceaseless strife,
With mind and heart as foes in fierce debate,
A quest for calm amidst the inner rife,
The heart's true strength decides the war's own fate.

For in this silent war, the heart shall reign,
Conquering the turmoil, breaking every chain.

33. The Lessons of Tears

Tears teach us truths the heart cannot disguise,
Revealing moments when our strength is weak,
They flow like torrents, falling from our eyes,
When patience wanes and solace we must seek.

Obstacles in life may not concede,
They journey with us like a steadfast sail,
Enduring as we face each pressing need,
An unmoved mover, through the stormy gale.

Our tears mark trials we are forced to bear,
Yet others' tears reflect their love so deep,
In their soft glow, a caring heart laid bare,
A sign of love and bonds that truly keep.

So heed the tears that fall in joy or strife,
They guide us through the pain and love in life.

34. The True Nature of Love

Our love sometimes lacks the grace we seek,
Its loveliness depends on who we choose,
To love someone who offers not a peak,
Can bring a lifetime's sorrow and abuse.

There are no strict rules that bind the heart,
Love knows no bounds of caste or creed,
Race or religion, age or status part,
These are but barriers that love can heed.

Yet loving one who's in another's arms,
And finds in them a joy that's true and bright,
Is not the essence of love's tender charms,
For love should be returned, pure and right.

So seek a heart that beats with yours in kind,
For love must be a bond, sincere and blind.

35. Transformation Through Love

You make me sad when I long to be bright,
Your memories linger when I try to cease,
My mind is restless, craving for respite,
No appetite remains when thoughts find peace.

My heart endures the weight of pain for you,
It bore no trials, once so light and free,
Now patience blooms where none before grew,
And anger fades, revealing truth to see.

Knowledge turns to wisdom through our past,
Callousness to sensitivity refined,
Ignorance to significance amassed,
Happiness to sweet pain, by love designed.

In you, I've changed and learned through love's deep flame,
A journey from pure joy to bittersweet name.

36. The Agony of Unfulfilled Love

Some kind of agony always moves within,
No one can name the precise pain it brings,
Yet heartache lingers where true solace thins,
Who will assuage such suffering, who sings?

Months and years drift by with no reprieve,
No lullaby to soothe the aching soul,
Death's embrace may not come to relieve,
The heart remains unquenched, its wounds unwhole.

Is it fortune to fall in love's deep snare?
Or is it curse to face such endless plight?
Life becomes a storm when love's not there,
A hurricane of grief without respite.

In love, the heart endures a cruel fate,
With no remedy to ease or to abate.

37. The Eternal Bond of Two Souls

The two wonderful souls were torn apart,
Their eyes no longer met, their paths unspun,
A sudden rift that shattered every heart,
Their parting was unplanned, though it begun.

Inside, they wept in silence, deep and still,
Their sorrow lingers, never truly fades,
That fateful day etched red, a void to fill,
A haunting memory that never shades.

Though physically apart, they remain,
In thought and spirit ever intertwined,
Their bond defies the fate, a subtle gain,
In minds and hearts, their unity aligned.

Together they have conquered time and space,
Their love endures, a constant, sacred grace.

38. The True Essence of Love

True love of a lady shines when he
Falls short of wealth, yet she stands by him,
A beacon through the storm, unwaveringly,
Her support a light, never growing dim.

True love of a man shows in the face
Of rejection, still his heart remains true,
His affection constant, no time to chase,
Even when romance is far from view.

Love is not measured by demands or gain,
Nor by the gifts or comforts it may bring,
It's found in giving, never in the chain,
Of expectations or the joys we cling.

True love unites two souls in sacred bond,
A blessing shared, beyond the worldly fond.

39. The Agony of Waiting

Waiting for someone is a woeful plight,
With idle hours and songs to soothe the soul,
Headphones in place, on sandstone waiting right,
Recalling memories, the time takes its toll.

Hours stretch on, yet she remains unseen,
Calls unanswered, silence fills the air,
The clock moves slow, the day's a weary scene,
As patience fades, replaced by deep despair.

Why must these moments stretch with such delay?
Do they not feel the anxious hope we bear?
Punctuality should be more than just a say,
It's a mark of respect and heartfelt care.

If sincerity and duty they embrace,
They'd ease our wait, and time would find its place.

40. The Soul's Enduring Pain

My soul has borne a pain beyond the words,
No magic phrase could capture its deep ache,
With every clash, my heart in silence stirred,
Tears flowing freely, for its own sake.

The flesh within grew hard as stone and brick,
Though wounds were felt, the blood did not emerge,
Cemented sorrow made the heart grow thick,
Yet love's warm ember still refused to purge.

Despite the trials, the soul retained its hope,
A flicker of light in the darkest night,
It dreams of rising and a future cope,
To mend the wounds and reclaim its might.

So through the pain, the heart remains alive,
With hope to heal and once again to thrive.

41. A Souvenir of Life's Transformation

The finest gift that life has ever brought
Was on the day our paths began to cross,
While commuting, in a moment caught,
My soul, once dull, began to sense the loss.

A change occurred I couldn't quite explain,
My heart, once still, awoke to vibrant beats,
A dormant spirit stirred from deep within,
In you, I found the joy that life completes.

Reflecting on the past, I see the shift,
From somber days to moments bright and new,
The miracles of change began to lift,
A fuller self, enriched by knowing you.

In thrilling hearts, such wonders come alive,
My soul and body dance, and I thrive.

42. The Rarest Eyes

The rarest eyes, in hidden beauty gleam,
Their splendor lies concealed from many sights.
Yet one who loves, can see beyond the dream,
The grace within those eyes' enchanting lights.

A radiant face, as if it holds the sun,
Absorbing all the world's most wondrous hues.
In gazing, joy is found by only one,
Who sees the soul that in those depths imbues.

Why did da Vinci choose his artful prize?
The Mona Lisa's gaze, so rich and deep,
Perhaps he knew of beauty's rarest guise,
A secret that in stillness softly sleeps.

In eyes so rare, true art and love are spun,
For beauty's heart is known by only one.

43. The Wounds of a Broken Heart

When heart is hurt, no balm can mend the pain,
Its depth a wound that time alone can heal.
No remedy can bring back joy again,
Nor soothe the ache that only time can seal.

A broken heart endures a darkened state,
Where sorrow breeds, and patience is the key.
In shadows cast by pressures that create
A hollow void where once was hope set free.

Though pleasure fades and weight of sorrow grows,
The healing comes in gentle, patient time.
For wounds of love are deepest when they close,
Yet peace returns as days begin to climb.

So bear the burden with a steady grace,
For healing comes, though slowly, in its place.

44. The Test of Time and Love

Two souls in love were once entwined in grace,
In fleeting moments, they were all the world.
Their hearts in sync, a perfect, tender place,
The models of love's banner, flags unfurled.

Yet fate, unkind, did cast its shadowed net,
And tore them from each other's warm embrace.
Though sorrow came, their bond was not to set,
For love grew stronger through its own distress.

As days unfolded, troubles took their toll,
Their hearts, once joined, now bore the weight of strife.
Blame marred the trust and frayed the love's pure goal,
And left them questioning the worth of life.

*Yet if the bond is true, love's strength will show,
For only through the test does real love grow.*

4o mini

45. The Trial of the Heart

In moments harsh, when condemnation falls,
For trembling hearts within the bond of love,
The pain of judgment strikes with bitter calls,
When none can grasp the truth from high above.

The world, divided, fails to comprehend
The raw sincerity of hearts distressed.
Instead, it casts aside and will not mend,
Denouncing those whose motives are repressed.

To punish those who've done no wrongful deed,
Yet bring them to account for what they bear,
Is more than wrong; it's cruel in its greed,
To judge the innocent with heavy care.

So let us temper justice with the grace,
And honor love's true worth in every case.

46. The Rose of Love

A red rose blooms in splendor, bright and rare,
A symbol pure of love's eternal flame.
Though fleeting in its bloom, beyond compare,
Its impact lasts, a timeless, cherished claim.

Presented with this rose, our hearts unfold,
In silent speech where ordinary words fall short.
Its petals whisper tales of love untold,
Transforming simple acts into grand court.

In every bloom, emotions find their voice,
A tender gesture etched in minds and hearts.
The rose transcends its form, making love's choice,
A cherished emblem as the soul imparts.

So let the rose be more than fleeting grace,
A token of the love we long embrace.

47. The Call for Change

When the heart whispers of a flaw unknown,
And warns of behavior not in line,
It's time to heed its call and not postpone,
For transformation must align with time.

Reflect upon your actions and their sway,
Does your conduct cause another's pain?
If so, embrace the chance to change your way,
And mend the harm with insight gained again.

Adapt to time's demands and shifting scene,
For growth requires a change in course and view.
To remain in a state of grace serene,
One must evolve, the old must make way for new.

So heed the heart's soft call to self-reflect,
And mold your ways to earn respect and love.

48. The Weight of Unyielding Pain

What is this pain, so deep and unrelenting?
It drags the heart, a burden hard to bear,
As if a heavy force is ever pressing,
A weight that time alone cannot repair.

The agony persists beyond the season,
Its shadows cling where solace once might grow,
I hoped it would dissolve with passing reason,
Yet still, the pain remains, and does not go.

Though wisdom offers guidance, clear and bright,
The struggle to embrace it proves so steep.
For even veterans in life's long fight
Find it's the heart's true challenge, not the speech.

So here I stand, with wisdom's lessons clear,
Yet still the ache persists, though time may steer.

49. The Melancholy of Unmet Affection

When attempts fall short in love's embrace,
A heartache rises like the ocean's swell,
The yearning waves in sorrow's endless chase,
A bitter, nameless pain none can dispel.

Why does the heart, so pure, face such disdain?
Why do the skies remain so dark and cold,
When every hope seems lost, in vain and pain,
And dreams of joy seem distant, tales untold?

Yet, as the sea retreats to kiss the shore,
New chances come to mend what's been forlorn,
Though once again the heart may ache and mourn,
The cycles of despair will reappear.

In time, as waves will reach and then recede,
We find our hearts will heal from every need.

50. When Fantasy Becomes Reality

In dreams, we yearn for cinematic scenes,
When life might play a part in wondrous tales,
A script of joy beyond our wildest dreams,
Where fantasy and real life intertwine.

If such a scene were truly to unfold,
The boundless joy would lift us to the skies,
A thrill so vivid, stories yet untold,
Would dance in hearts with wonder and surprise.

These moments rare, like stars that briefly shine,
A glimpse of magic in our everyday,
When dreams and life's great canvas intertwine,
And fill our souls with euphoria's sway.

Such moments, fleeting, etch themselves in time,
A cherished thrill, where dreams and truth align.

Made in the USA
Monee, IL
03 May 2026